T0193446

Adopted by a King

IVA HENDON

Archway Publishing books may be ordered through booksellers or by contacting:

Archway Publishing
1663 Liberty Drive
Bloomington, IN 47403
www.archwaypublishing.com
844-669-3957

Scripture taken from the King James Version of the Bible.

Interior Image Credit: Lona Courington

ISBN: 978-1-6657-3095-2 (sc)
ISBN: 978-1-6657-3096-9 (hc)
ISBN: 978-1-6657-3097-6 (e)

Print information available on the last page.

Archway Publishing rev. date: 10/25/2022

To my family and friends who helped me in so many ways to get this book to print, thank you from the bottom of my heart. I couldn't have done it without you. To my sister, Lona, who illustrated for me and spent endless hours helping me technologically, I love you and owe you big time. To our great God, who drew us to Himself, loved us, and adopted us as his own, my deepest gratitude and undying devotion.

This book is dedicated to my grandchildren: Ethan, Tristan, Wyatt, Avery, Charlotte, Phillip, Marcus, Ginny, Thomas, Liam, James Sanford, and Juniper, as well as Judah Christian who is on the way and several who await us in heaven and, hopefully, many more yet to join us on this journey.

ADOPTED BY A KING

"Rejoice in the Lord alway: and again I say rejoice." (KJV Philippians 4:4)

It's a celebration! Come; let's dance and sing!

I'm a follower of Jesus, adopted by a king!

My heart was stirred
inside me; I trusted
and believed.

"So, then, faith comes by hearing, and hearing by the word of God." (KJV Romans 10:17)

My sins, now all forgiven, I'm free; let's dance and sing!

My journey's an adventure; who knows what life may bring?

When hills and dales get rough, I'll talk to Daddy, Abba, King!

"What time I am afraid, I will trust in thee." (KJV Psalm 56:3)

His spirit lives inside me; I have no need to fear.

I know He's here to guide me; when I call
Him, He draws near

It's a celebration! Come; let's dance and sing!

I'm a follower of Jesus, and loved by Him,
THE KING!

"All power is given unto me in heaven and in earth." (Jesus, KJV Matt. 28-18b)

"Go ye therefore and teach all nations, baptizing them in the name of the Father, and of the Son, and of the Holy Ghost: teaching them to observe whatsoever things I have commanded you." (KJV Matt. 28:19-20a)

"and, lo, I am with you alway,"
(KJV Matt.28:20b)

"even unto the end of the world."

(KJV" Matt. 28: 20c)

Iva Hendon is a devout Christian who has taken great joy in seeing her descendants become followers of Jesus. She is an educator with a BA in SPE-MR from the University of Alabama and a Master's degree in Special Education/Learning Disabilities. As an empty nester, Hendon spends her time, outside of family, serving as Action Groups Director for Alabama Eagle Forum, a Christian, pro-family policy organization that advocates and lobbies for conservative values.

Lona Courington is a retired nonprofit executive who is rediscovering her art. She holds a BFA in painting and graphic design from the University of Alabama.

Printed in the United States
by Baker & Taylor Publisher Services